INSIDE THE NFL

LOS ANGELES RAMS

by Luke Hanlon

Abdo & Daughters
MIDDLE GRADE NONFICTION

An imprint of Abdo Publishing
abdobooks.com

ABDOBOOKS.COM

Published by Abdo Publishing, a division of ABDO, PO Box 398166, Minneapolis, Minnesota 55439.

Printed in China.
052025
092025

THIS BOOK CONTAINS RECYCLED MATERIALS

Cover Photos: Lauren Leigh Bacho/Getty Images Sport/Getty Images (Puka Nacua); Ryan Kang/Getty Images Sport/Getty Images (Aaron Donald)
Interior Photos: Kevin C. Cox/Getty Images Sport/Getty Images, 4–5, 10, 11, 61 (bottom right); Steph Chambers/Getty Images Sport/Getty Images, 6; Katelyn Mulcahy/Getty Images Sport/Getty Images, 7; Gregory Shamus/Getty Images Sport/Getty Images, 8–9; Abdo Publishing, 12–13, 58; AP Images, 14–15, 18, 19, 20, 60 (bottom left); Vic Stein/Getty Images Sport/Getty Images, 16, 21, 27; Bettmann/Getty Images, 17, 28; Harold P. Matosian/AP Images, 22; Phil Bath/Los Angeles Times/Getty Images, 23; Tony Tomsic/AP Images, 24–25; James Flores/Getty Images Sport/Getty Images, 26; Focus on Sport/Getty Images, 30, 32, 60 (top), 60 (bottom right); Peter Read Miller/AP Images, 31; Robert Riger/Getty Images Sport/Getty Images, 33; George Rose/Getty Images Sport/Getty Images, 34–35; David Madison/Getty Images Sport/Getty Images, 36, 63; Mark Avery/AP Images, 37; Mitchell Layton/Getty Images Sport/Getty Images, 38; Al Bello/Allsport/Getty Images Sport/Getty Images, 39; James A. Finley/AP Images, 40; Tom DiPace/AP Images, 41 (top), 42, 47, 61 (top left), 61 (bottom left); Wade Payne/AP Images, 41 (bottom); Paul Spinelli/NFL Photos/AP Images, 43; John Gaps III/AP Images, 44–45; Focus on Sport/Getty Images Sport/Getty Images, 46; Allen Kee/AP Images, 48–49; Albert Dickson/Sporting News Archive/Getty Images, 50; Harry How/Getty Images Sport/Getty Images, 51, 54; Robin Alam/Corbis/Icon Sportswire/Getty Images, 52; Greg Trott/AP Images, 53; Scott Varley/Digital First Media/Torranco Daily Breeze/MediaNews Group/Getty Images, 55; Margaret Bowles/AP Images, 56, 61 (top right); Rob Carr/Getty Images Sport/Getty Images, 57; Cooper Neill/Getty Images Sport/Getty Images, 59

Editor: Haley Williams
Series Designer: Laura Graphenteen
Production Designer: Ebonee Estrella

Library of Congress Control Number: 2024948508

Publisher's Cataloging-in-Publication Data

Names: Hanlon, Luke, author.
Title: Los Angeles Rams / by Luke Hanlon
Description: Minneapolis, Minnesota: Abdo Publishing, 2026 | Series: Inside the NFL | Includes online resources and index.
Identifiers: ISBN 9781098296803 (lib. bdg.) | ISBN 9798384919322 (ebook)
Subjects: LCSH: Los Angeles Rams (Football team: 2016-)--Juvenile literature. | National Football League--Juvenile literature. | Football teams--Juvenile literature. | American football--Juvenile literature.
Classification: DDC 796.333--dc23

CONTENTS

Los Angeles Rams quarterback Matthew Stafford, *back left*, prepares to start a play during Super Bowl LVI in February 2022.

CHAPTER 1

HOLLYWOOD ENDING

Los Angeles Rams head coach Sean McVay faced a crucial decision. With five minutes left in Super Bowl LVI on February 13, 2022, his team trailed the Cincinnati Bengals 20–16. The Rams had the ball, but they faced fourth-and-one from their own 30-yard line. The safe play would have been to punt the ball away and hope the Rams' defense could quickly get it back. Instead, McVay put his trust in star wide receiver Cooper Kupp to keep the drive alive.

Before the snap, Rams quarterback Matthew Stafford sent Kupp sprinting across the backfield from the left. In a quick motion, Stafford took the ball and handed it off to Kupp for a running play. Kupp raced toward the outside, but a Cincinnati defender had pushed into the backfield. This meant Kupp's path around the edge was blocked.

Receiver Cooper Kupp (10) caught eight passes in the Super Bowl.

Quickly adjusting, the speedy receiver cut back inside, escaped a defender, and burst up the field for a 7-yard gain and a first down. Because of Kupp's quick decision, the Rams' offense continued marching on.

BREAKFAST CLUB

The foundations of that play between Stafford and Kupp had been established throughout the season. Kupp was a rising star in Los Angeles. In 2021, the Rams paired him with one of the league's best passers when they traded for Stafford. All season, the duo met early at the team's practice facility to go over their offensive game plan while eating breakfast. Those meetings helped Stafford and Kupp blossom into one of the most unstoppable quarterback-wide receiver combos in the National Football League (NFL).

Kupp's crisp route running paired perfectly with Stafford's strong, accurate arm. Whenever the Rams needed a big play, Stafford would look for Kupp. With 145 catches, 1,947 receiving yards, and 16 receiving touchdowns, Kupp became the first player in 16 years to lead the NFL in all three categories. More importantly, Stafford and Kupp led the Rams to a 12–5 record that season. With three more wins in the playoffs, the team reached its second Super Bowl in four seasons.

HOME-FIELD ADVANTAGE

The Los Angeles Rams moved into SoFi Stadium in 2020. At $5 billion, it was the NFL's most expensive and state-of-the-art stadium. The NFL chose it as the host site for Super Bowl LVI. When the Rams reached the championship after the 2021 regular season, they became just the second team to play in the Super Bowl at their home stadium. The Tampa Bay Buccaneers were the first to do so when they won the year before.

Two Rams fans show off their outfits before Super Bowl LVI.

CLUTCH CONNECTION

Kupp's fourth-down run kept the Rams' offense on the field, but the team still had to travel 63 yards to reach the end zone.

With Los Angeles struggling to run all game, McVay kept the ball in Stafford's hands. Over the next nine plays, the Rams passed eight times. The biggest play went to Kupp, a 22-yard connection with just over three minutes to go.

With 1:47 remaining, the Rams faced third-and-goal from Cincinnati's 8-yard line. Once again, Stafford targeted Kupp. This time, a Cincinnati defender cut off the receiver's route and

Stafford, *right*, threw for 283 yards against the Cincinnati Bengals.

batted the pass out of the air. Instead of facing fourth down, though, the Rams got a break when the Bengals were called for defensive holding. The penalty gave Los Angeles a first down. Three plays later, the Rams still hadn't reached the end zone. But they caught another break when a Cincinnati pass interference penalty gave the Rams another first down. Los Angeles faced second-and-goal from the 1-yard line with 1:29 remaining.

The shortest route to the end zone was up the middle. Cincinnati bunched nine defenders right on the line of scrimmage to prevent that. This left a single defender on each of the two Los Angeles receivers lined up on the right side of the offensive formation. When Stafford received the snap, he looked to his right and saw Bengals cornerback Eli Apple covering Kupp on the outside. That was the matchup the quarterback was looking for.

Kupp stutter-stepped to try to shake free from Apple as Stafford lofted a pass to the right side of the end zone. The receiver kept his eyes on the ball the entire time. With Apple tightly covering him, Kupp spun his body around, leaped, and hauled in the touchdown.

Facing the biggest drive of the season, Stafford and Kupp came through to give the Rams a 23–20 lead with 1:25 left. That proved to be the game-winning score. The victory gave the Rams just their second Super Bowl title. When talking after the game about that final offensive drive, McVay said, "You put the ball in your best players' hands when it matters the most. That's what we did."

"YOU PUT THE BALL IN YOUR BEST PLAYERS' HANDS WHEN IT MATTERS THE MOST. THAT'S WHAT WE DID."

—SEAN MCVAY

Stafford recorded three passing touchdowns in Super Bowl LVI.

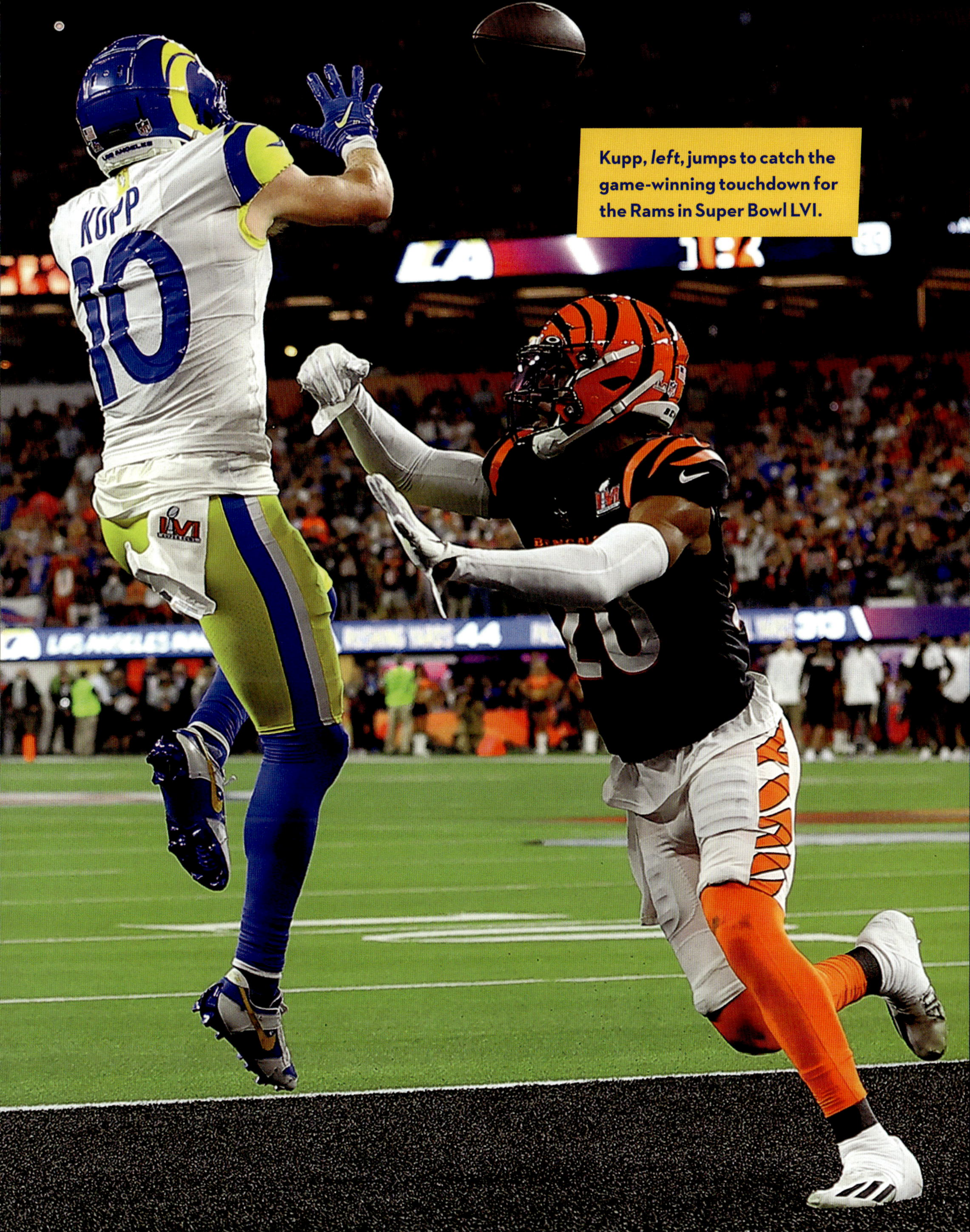

Kupp, *left*, jumps to catch the game-winning touchdown for the Rams in Super Bowl LVI.

NFL TEAMS MAP

NFC

NFC EAST

- DALLAS COWBOYS
- NEW YORK GIANTS
- PHILADELPHIA EAGLES
- WASHINGTON COMMANDERS

NFC WEST

- ARIZONA CARDINALS
- LOS ANGELES RAMS
- SAN FRANCISCO 49ERS
- SEATTLE SEAHAWKS

NFC NORTH

- CHICAGO BEARS
- DETROIT LIONS
- GREEN BAY PACKERS
- MINNESOTA VIKINGS

NFC SOUTH

- ATLANTA FALCONS
- CAROLINA PANTHERS
- NEW ORLEANS SAINTS
- TAMPA BAY BUCCANEERS

AFC

AFC EAST

- BUFFALO BILLS
- MIAMI DOLPHINS
- NEW ENGLAND PATRIOTS
- NEW YORK JETS

AFC WEST

- DENVER BRONCOS
- KANSAS CITY CHIEFS
- LAS VEGAS RAIDERS
- LOS ANGELES CHARGERS

AFC NORTH

- BALTIMORE RAVENS
- CINCINNATI BENGALS
- CLEVELAND BROWNS
- PITTSBURGH STEELERS

AFC SOUTH

- HOUSTON TEXANS
- INDIANAPOLIS COLTS
- JACKSONVILLE JAGUARS
- TENNESSEE TITANS

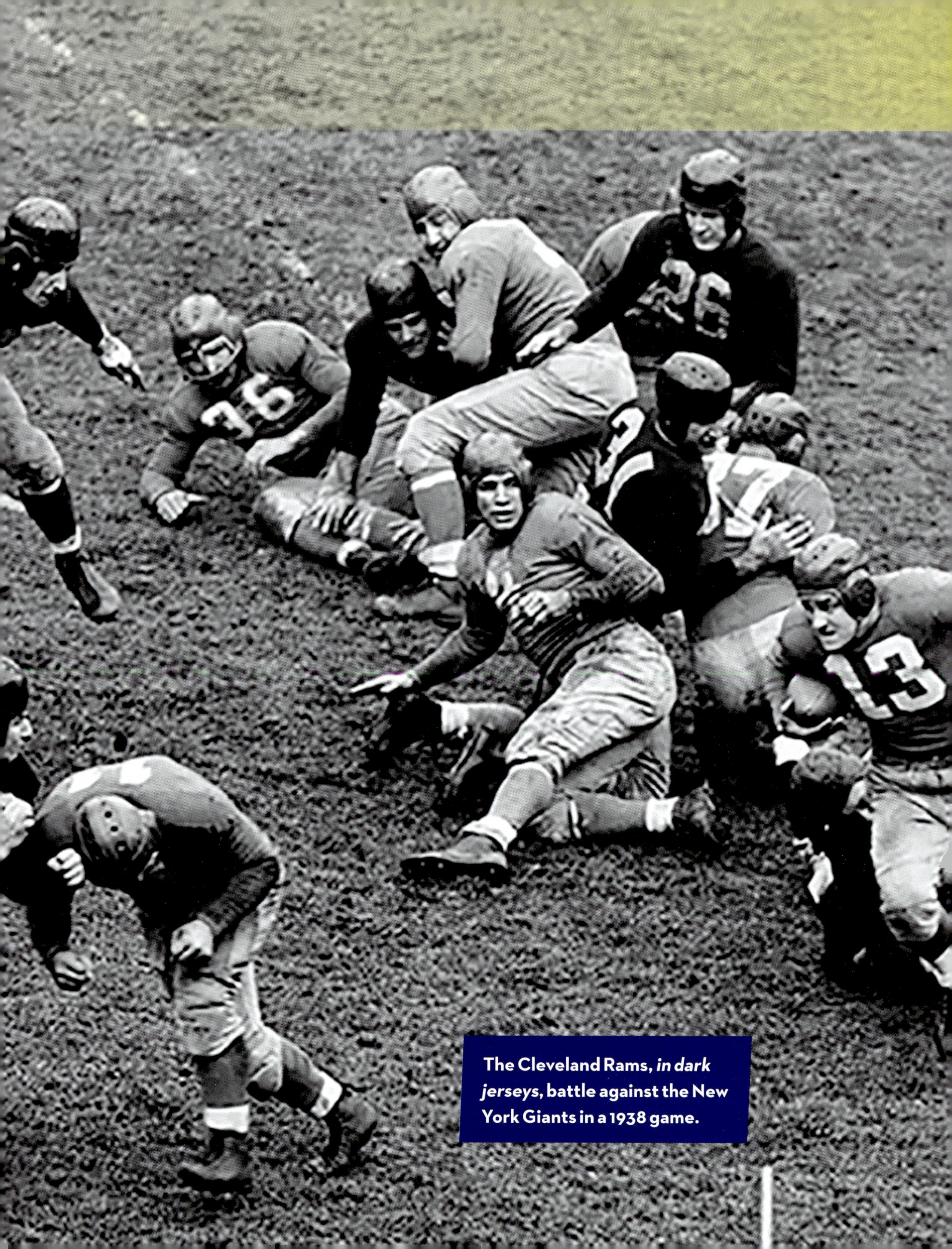

The Cleveland Rams, *in dark jerseys*, battle against the New York Giants in a 1938 game.

CHAPTER 2

OHIO ORIGINS

The history of the Rams started more than 2,000 miles (3,200 km) east of Los Angeles. In 1936, lawyer Homer Marshman and former Ohio State football player Damon Wetzel founded the Rams in Cleveland. Wetzel played on and coached the team, leading the Rams to a 5–2–2 record in the upstart American Football League (AFL). After just one year in the AFL, the Rams joined the more prosperous NFL in 1937 with the hopes of making more money.

In their first year in the NFL, the Rams struggled. The league proved to be far more competitive than the AFL. In 1941, Marshman sold the Rams to businessman Dan Reeves. But the new management didn't help turn the team around. In their first seven years in the NFL, the Rams didn't record a single winning season.

Quarterback Bob Waterfield threw for 1,609 yards during his rookie season in 1945.

As the losses piled up, fan interest in the Rams dwindled.

One player eventually helped to turn things around for Cleveland. In the 1944 NFL Draft, the Rams selected Bob Waterfield. The young quarterback from the University of California Los Angeles (UCLA) was ahead of his time. Most offenses in this era relied on running the ball to gain yards. While the Rams still ran the ball in 1945, Waterfield also tore up opposing defenses with long passes down the field.

Waterfield took the league by storm and led the NFL in touchdown passes that season. Having All-Pro wide receiver Jim Benton helped Waterfield. On Thanksgiving Day in 1945, Benton became the first player in NFL history to record more than 300 receiving yards in a game, as he hauled in 10 catches for 303 yards. The dangerous duo of Waterfield and Benton led the Rams to a 9–1 record and secured a spot in the NFL Championship Game. There, Waterfield tossed two touchdowns, with one going to Benton, to lead the Rams to a 15–14 victory over Washington.

CALIFORNIA DREAMING

In 1945, a crowd of more than 32,000 fans filled Cleveland Municipal Stadium to watch the Rams win their first NFL title. But crowds that big had become a rarity for the Rams, even with their success on the field. The team consistently lost money each season. To make matters worse, a new pro football team, the Cleveland Browns, was about to play its first season in 1946. Even though the Rams had just won a championship, Reeves feared the Browns would make it hard to attract more fans, so he pushed to move his team to Los Angeles.

The other NFL owners were upset by the idea. At that time, every NFL team was located east of the Mississippi River, so none of the owners wanted their team to travel thousands of miles for an away game. However, Reeves wouldn't take no for an answer. With the Browns about to start play, Reeves was determined to get the Rams to Los Angeles in 1946.

When the move became official, the Rams became the first major sports franchise to play on the West Coast. However, the team faced one more roadblock. At that time, the NFL was segregated. Before the Rams could use the Los Angeles Memorial Coliseum, the city

Wide receiver Jim Benton (49) led the NFL in receiving yards in both 1945 and 1946.

The Los Angeles Memorial Coliseum opened in 1923.

required the team to sign a Black player. So Reeves signed former UCLA stars Kenny Washington and Woody Strode, making them the first Black players to compete in the NFL since 1933.

With a championship-caliber roster in place, the Rams looked to be in a great position to captivate Los Angeles. However, in 1946, the Los Angeles Dons professional football team also started playing in the new All-America Football Conference (AAFC). With another pro team in town, the Rams struggled to fill the stands in their home stadium. After losing money each year in Cleveland, Reeves began taking bigger financial losses in Los Angeles.

DOUBLE TROUBLE

After winning six games in each of their first three seasons in Los Angeles, the Rams needed a boost. They got one in the

Defensive back Kenny Washington (13) and end Woody Strode (34) pose with other Rams players in 1946.

1949 draft when the team selected quarterback Norm Van Brocklin in the fourth round. The team still had Waterfield, who remained the starter. But Van Brocklin also played. Both quarterbacks were eventually inducted into the Pro Football Hall of Fame.

The Rams finished 8–2–2 in 1949 to secure the West Division title and a trip to the NFL Championship Game. Both Waterfield and Van Brocklin played in the game, but neither quarterback could get anything going against the stingy Philadelphia Eagles' defense. The Rams were shut out 14–0.

The timing of the Rams' run to the title game couldn't have worked out any better. After the 1949 season, the AAFC folded, leaving the Rams as the only professional football team in town. The team was ready to take advantage of that and win over new fans.

Waterfield and Van Brocklin had a pair of excellent receivers to work with. Tom Fears was one of the best deep threats in football. Speedster Elroy Hirsch had a distinct running style. He seemed to twist all directions while taking his long strides, earning him the nickname "Crazy Legs." Both pass catchers put up huge numbers. With talent all over the field, the Rams boasted the league's highest-scoring offense three years in a row starting in 1950.

Waterfield and Van Brocklin each started six games that season. But it didn't matter who played under center. The Rams returned to the championship while putting up an NFL-record 38.8 points per game. For the title game, the team traveled to its old home in Cleveland to take on the Browns, who had joined the NFL that season. While Los Angeles had split time between quarterbacks all season, Waterfield played almost the entire championship game. He threw for 312 yards, but the Rams fell short. Despite Los Angeles having the lead going into the fourth quarter, Cleveland rallied to win 30–28 on a field goal with just seconds to play.

Before Week 1 of the 1951 season, Waterfield suffered an injury. Van Brocklin stepped

Quarterback Norm Van Brocklin threw 118 touchdowns in nine seasons with the Rams.

Wide receiver Elroy Hirsch (40) led the NFL in receptions, receiving yards, and touchdowns in 1951.

in and was dominant against the New York Yanks, throwing five touchdown passes and for an NFL-record 554 yards. But Van Brocklin struggled the following week against the Browns, and Waterfield came on in relief. Waterfield remained the starter for the rest of the regular season.

After securing another division title in 1951, the Rams hosted the Browns in the NFL title game. Waterfield started the game, but he threw two interceptions, and Rams coach Joe Stydahar benched him. Van Brocklin replaced Waterfield and proved to be the hero. With the score tied 17–17 midway through the fourth quarter, Van Brocklin delivered a perfect pass down the field to hit Fears in stride. Fears ran to the end zone for a 73-yard, game-winning touchdown. After the game, the receiver said, "That was the best thrown pass I ever caught in my life."

"THAT WAS THE BEST THROWN PASS I EVER CAUGHT IN MY LIFE."

—TOM FEARS

HISTORIC ROOKIE

Before the 1952 season, US Army veteran Dick "Night Train" Lane went to Los Angeles to work at an aircraft plant. Each day, he'd pass the Rams' office on his way to work. One day, Lane decided to stop in to try out for the team. Initially, he attempted to play on offense as a wide receiver. But head coach Joe Stydahar decided Lane would make a better defensive back. That decision quickly paid off. In 1952, Lane racked up 14 interceptions. More than 70 years later, no player has recorded more interceptions in a single NFL season.

In 1952, Dick Lane returned two of his 14 interceptions for touchdowns.

QUARTERBACK CONTROVERSY

The Rams continued rotating their superstar quarterbacks through the 1952 season. But when Waterfield retired after that season, Van Brocklin finally had the job to himself. The Rams failed to make the playoffs in his first two years as a starter. But Van Brocklin made the most of his opportunity and led the NFL in passing yards in 1954.

Before the 1955 season, Los Angeles hired Sid Gillman as its new head coach. The Rams already threw the ball a lot, but Gillman wanted his offense to pass the ball even more. He would often say, "The big play comes with the pass." And Gillman had the perfect quarterback to execute his plans. With Van Brocklin airing the ball out, the Rams reached another NFL title game, but they fell to the Browns 38–14.

Rams players carry head coach Sid Gillman off the field after a win in 1955.

Despite the successful season, Van Brocklin and Gillman were not always on the same page. The two often bickered over the team's offensive game plan. Sometimes during games, Van Brocklin would ignore Gillman's play calls and call a different play.

By the end of the 1957 season, the relationship between the head coach and quarterback had completely fallen apart. Van Brocklin said he wouldn't play another game for the Rams as long as Gillman was the coach. So before the 1958 season, the Rams traded Van Brocklin to the Eagles.

Defensive end Deacon Jones recorded 20 or more sacks in three different seasons with the Rams.

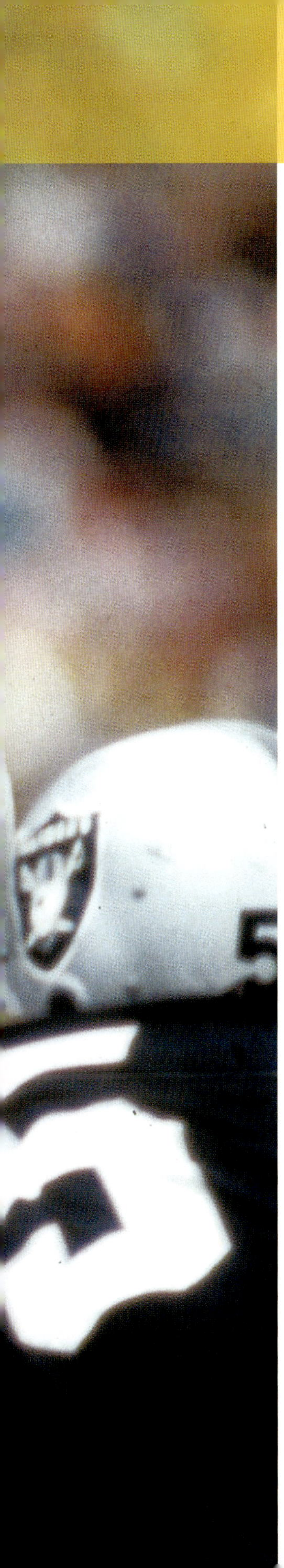

CHAPTER 3

SHIFTING TO DEFENSE

AFTER HAVING THE LEAGUE'S BEST OFFENSE THROUGHOUT THE 1950S, the Rams became known for their defense during the 1960s. In the 1961 NFL Draft, the Rams selected defensive end Deacon Jones. Then in the 1962 draft, the team chose defensive tackle Merlin Olsen with the third overall pick. The two linemen became the anchors of the Rams' defense for years to come.

Standing at 6 foot, 5 inches and weighing 272 pounds, Jones could move as fast as many running backs and wide receivers. He also had the power to move offensive linemen out of his way with his signature head slap. When rushing the passer, Jones would hit his blocker in the helmet to stun him. Then Jones could easily run past him to get to the opposing quarterback.

The NFL eventually banned the head slap, but Jones used it effectively throughout his Hall of Fame career.

Having Olsen on the inside of the line helped, too. Teams often needed two offensive linemen to block the super strong Olsen. Despite battling on the line of scrimmage every week, Olsen missed only two games during his 15-year career with the Rams.

Jones and Olsen teamed up with Pro Bowl defensive end Lamar Lundy, who had been with the Rams since 1957. Then in 1963, the Rams added to their depth of talent by trading for defensive tackle Rosey Grier. Together, Jones, Olsen, Lundy, and Grier were known as "the Fearsome Foursome."

Defensive tackle Merlin Olsen (74) made the Pro Bowl in 14 of his 15 seasons in the NFL.

The four linemen matched perfectly with one another, and they helped the Rams improve on defense throughout the 1960s. Hiring defensive-minded head coach George Allen in 1966 helped as well. Los Angeles had suffered seven straight losing seasons, but with Allen coaching the

Quarterback Roman Gabriel, *left*, played 11 seasons with the Rams from 1962 to 1972.

Fearsome Foursome, the Rams boasted one of the league's best defenses. Even when Grier suffered a career-ending injury before the 1967 season, the Rams' defense didn't fall off. Instead, Allen traded for Pro Bowl defensive tackle Roger Brown, and he created a new Fearsome Foursome alongside Jones, Olsen, and Lundy.

BITTER COLD

Everything came together for the Rams in 1967. With several star players on defense, Los Angeles allowed the fewest points in the NFL that year. And veteran quarterback Roman Gabriel led the league's best offense. The Rams ended the regular season on an eight-game winning streak and rolled into the playoffs for the first time in 12 years.

In the divisional-round game against the Green Bay Packers, Gabriel hit wide receiver Bernie Casey with a 29-yard touchdown pass to put the Rams up 7–0 in the first quarter. The early lead gave Los Angeles fans hope for a deep playoff run. However, playing in freezing temperatures, the Los Angeles offense halted from there. The Packers handed the Rams a 28–7 loss.

Allen kept the Rams competitive for the rest of the 1960s. Gabriel provided consistent quarterback play, and the Fearsome Foursome punished opposing offenses. In 1969, Gabriel could seemingly do no wrong. In an era when quarterbacks routinely turned the ball over, Gabriel threw a league-leading 24 touchdowns and tossed only seven interceptions. He won the NFL's Most Valuable Player (MVP) Award that year.

Gabriel, *right*, goes to pass in the playoff game between the Rams and Minnesota Vikings in December 1969.

Led by Gabriel, the Rams started the year 11-0. However, they ended the regular season on a three-game losing streak, forcing them to travel in the first round of the playoffs to take on the Minnesota Vikings. The Rams handled the cold weather better than they had two years earlier. Gabriel threw two touchdowns to give the Rams a 17-7 lead at halftime. But the Vikings shut down the Rams in the second half and stormed back to win 23-20.

After the heartbreaking loss to Minnesota, Los Angeles began to fade. The Rams missed the playoffs in 1970, and after the season, they fired Allen. During his time as head coach, Allen often traded high draft picks for veteran players. Once he was gone, the Rams changed course and attempted to build a new roster through the draft. Shortly after the 1971 season, the team traded Jones to the San Diego Chargers for three picks. Then before the 1973 season, the Rams traded Gabriel for more picks. With so many of the Rams' longtime leaders on offense and defense moving on, a new era was beginning in Los Angeles.

TRADING TEAMS

After Dan Reeves died in 1971, the Rams needed a new team owner. Chicago businessman Robert Irsay bought the team, but he didn't own it for long. In 1972, Carroll Rosenbloom, who was the owner of the Baltimore Colts, called Irsay. Rosenbloom proposed a straight trade of the two franchises, and Irsay agreed. Irsay became the owner of the Colts, and Rosenbloom became the owner of the Rams. In 1979, Rosenbloom suddenly passed away, and his wife, Georgia Frontiere, took over as the owner of the Rams.

BACK IN THE SPOTLIGHT

Heading into the 1973 season, the Rams seemed to be in the middle of a rebuild. However, new head coach Chuck Knox didn't think so. He believed the Rams had enough talent to win right away. On offense, he turned to second-year running back Lawrence McCutcheon. As the go-to back in the Rams' run-heavy offense, McCutcheon ran for 1,386 yards and helped the team score an NFL-best 388 points that year.

On defense, the Rams selected defensive end Jack Youngblood in the first round of the 1971 NFL Draft. After learning from Jones during his first two seasons, Youngblood became a full-time starter in 1973. He carried on the tradition of the Fearsome Foursome by recording 10 or more sacks in eight different seasons with the Rams.

The Rams took the league by storm and finished with a 12–2 record in 1973. However, they lost in the first round of the playoffs to the Dallas Cowboys, who had been one of the best teams in the National Football Conference (NFC) that year. Then from 1974 to 1976, the Rams made it to the NFC Championship Game every season. But each time, the Rams lost to either the Cowboys or the Vikings. After the Vikings ended the Rams' season in the first round of the 1977 postseason, Los Angeles owner Carroll Rosenbloom became fed up with the playoff losses and fired Knox.

Ahead of the 1978 season, Rosenbloom hired Ray Malavasi as the Rams' head coach. Malavasi had served as the team's defensive

In 14 seasons with the Rams, defensive end Jack Youngblood had 151 1/2 sacks.

Due to the field conditions, the December 1977 playoff game between the Rams and Vikings was called "the Mud Bowl."

coordinator since 1973. However, he didn't lead to a different result as head coach. The Rams won their division again, but their season ended with a 28–0 loss to the Cowboys in the NFC title game.

PLAYING THROUGH PAIN

By 1979, the Rams seemed to be running on fumes. During the season, 19 players suffered significant injuries, including three of the team's four captains. However, Youngblood, the only healthy captain, racked up a league-leading 18 sacks. His efforts helped lift the Rams to a 9–7 record and a seventh straight division title.

The Rams opened the playoffs in Dallas against the Cowboys. But in the first half, Youngblood broke his left leg. Knowing how shorthanded his team already was, the defensive end convinced team doctors to let him play through the injury. Despite being in intense pain, he recorded a key late-game sack to seal a 21–19 victory for the Rams.

Youngblood continued to play on his broken leg the following week in the NFC Championship Game. His toughness helped inspire a strong defensive performance from his teammates as the Rams won 9–0 over the Tampa Bay Buccaneers to clinch Los Angeles's first trip to the Super Bowl, which had been introduced in the 1966 season.

The Rams didn't have to travel far to get there. Super Bowl XIV took place at the Rose Bowl in Pasadena, California, which was just 15 miles (24 km) down the road from the Coliseum. A record 103,985 fans filled the stadium to watch the underdog Rams take

The Rams' defense swarms a Pittsburgh Steelers player during Super Bowl XIV in January 1980.

Running back Lawrence McCutcheon (30) looks for an open receiver during Super Bowl XIV.

on the Pittsburgh Steelers, who were playing for their fourth Super Bowl title in six years.

Despite the Rams' inexperience in the big game, they hung with the Steelers. At halftime, Los Angeles held a 13–10 lead. Even after Pittsburgh went ahead early in the third quarter, the Rams wouldn't go away. On their next drive, the Rams ran a halfback pass, and McCutcheon tossed a 24-yard touchdown to wide receiver Ron Smith to put the Rams back in front 19–17.

The Los Angeles defense stepped up and intercepted Steelers star quarterback Terry Bradshaw on Pittsburgh's next two drives. However, the Rams couldn't capitalize on the turnovers. Bradshaw bounced back in the fourth quarter and led two touchdown drives to put the Steelers ahead. The Rams' unlikely run to the Super Bowl ended in a 31–19 loss. While fans in Los Angeles dealt with the lost opportunity, they'd soon find out that the team that had called the city its home for more than three decades would be leaving.

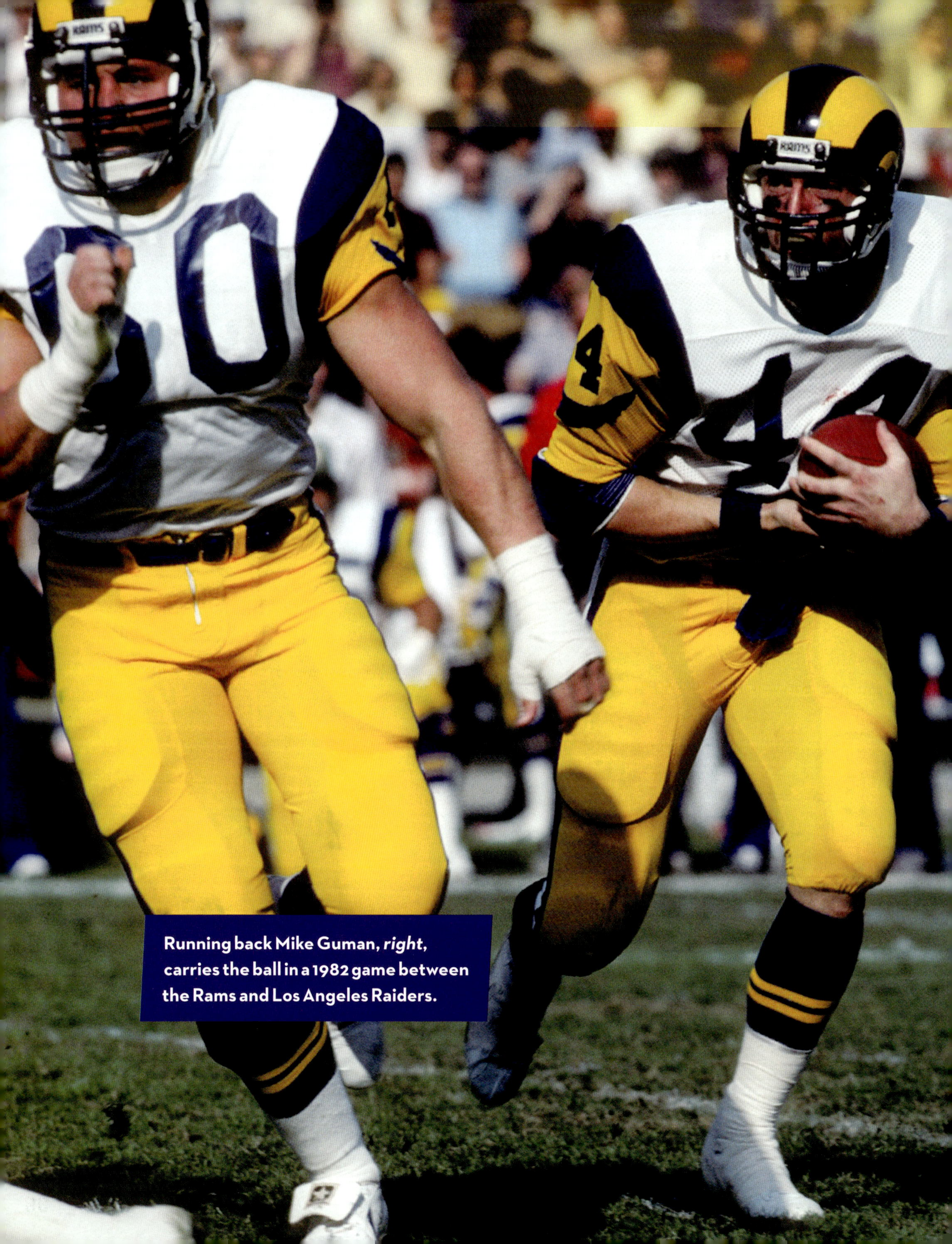

Running back Mike Guman, *right*, carries the ball in a 1982 game between the Rams and Los Angeles Raiders.

CHAPTER 4

THE GREATEST SHOW ON TURF

WHEN THE RAMS TOOK THE FIELD IN 1980 LOOKING TO MAKE IT BACK to the Super Bowl, they did so in a different stadium. That year, the Rams moved out of the Coliseum and into Anaheim Stadium more than 30 miles (48 km) south of Los Angeles. Two years later, the Oakland Raiders moved to Los Angeles and began playing in the Coliseum. With these changes, fan interest in the Rams began to decline.

The fans that stuck with the Rams had plenty to be excited about, though. In the 1983 NFL Draft, the Rams selected Eric Dickerson, who became one of the most electric players in the league. The 6-foot-3-inch, 220-pound running back seemed to glide effortlessly on the field. Dickerson set NFL rookie records with 1,808 rushing yards and 18 touchdown runs.

In 1984, no opposing defense could stop Dickerson. By Week 14, he had rushed for 1,792 yards, putting him 211 yards away from the NFL single-season rushing record. The following week, the Rams faced the Houston Oilers. Before the 1983 draft, Dickerson, a Houston native, said he didn't want to play for the Oilers because he didn't see them as being competitive anytime soon. So leading up to the game, some Houston players downplayed Dickerson's season, saying his offensive line was the only reason he'd racked up so many yards.

Dickerson made sure to prove those players wrong. He gashed Houston for big gains throughout the game. As Dickerson inched toward the record, Rams fans roared every time he touched the ball.

Late in the fourth quarter, Dickerson needed 6 yards to break the record. He took a handoff and juked a defender to avoid a tackle. By the time the Oilers dragged him down, Dickerson had gained 9 yards to give him the record. Dickerson's teammates swarmed him to celebrate, while the home fans roared for their star running back. Dickerson finished the season with 2,105 rushing yards.

With Dickerson pacing the offense, the Rams made

Running back Eric Dickerson led the NFL in rushing yards in three of his four full seasons with the Rams.

Dickerson shows off the ball he carried to break the NFL single-season rushing record in 1984.

the playoffs for four straight seasons from 1983 to 1986. However, the team never made it past the NFC Championship Game. During this run, Dickerson demanded more money from the Rams, but the team wouldn't sign him to a new contract. Los Angeles eventually traded Dickerson during the 1987 season. Without a star player to watch, fewer fans showed up for Rams games.

MOVING OUT

Starting in 1990, the Rams' on-field performance sharply declined. With each losing season, attendance continued to decrease. By 1994, the Rams had the lowest attendance in the NFL.

With a lack of interest from fans in Los Angeles, and the city not offering to build a new stadium, Rams owner Georgia Frontiere proposed to move the team to her hometown of St. Louis. When the other NFL owners voted on the move in March 1995, 21 out of the 30 voted against it. However, Frontiere threatened to sue the league for billions of dollars if the move wasn't approved. The owners held another vote a month later, and this time, 23 owners voted for the move.

Dick Vermeil coached 15 years in the NFL and won 120 games.

Moving to a new city did not boost the Rams' performance on the field, though. The team suffered losing seasons in 1995 and 1996. So before the 1997 season, the Rams made a bold move by hiring Dick Vermeil as the team's head coach. While Vermeil had led the Philadelphia Eagles to their first Super Bowl appearance after the 1980 regular season, he hadn't coached in the NFL in 15 years. Even so, the Rams were hoping he would be the coach to help turn the team around.

UNKNOWN BACKUP

At first, the Rams didn't improve under Vermeil. The team had losing years in both 1997 and 1998. Despite All-Pro players such as wide receiver Isaac Bruce and left tackle Orlando Pace, the team suffered from poor quarterback play.

So ahead of the 1999 season, the Rams signed strong-armed quarterback Trent Green as a free agent. Then later in the offseason, they traded for running back Marshall Faulk, who had led the NFL in total yards the previous season while playing for the Indianapolis Colts. The Rams also selected wide receiver Torry Holt in the 1999 draft. Vermeil entered the season confident his Rams were about to turn the corner.

However, Green suffered a season-ending knee injury during a preseason game, and the Rams turned to untested backup quarterback Kurt Warner. Few NFL fans knew anything about Warner. He attended Northern Iowa and didn't start a game until his senior year. After going undrafted in 1994, Warner worked in a local grocery store while trying to keep his football dreams alive. He played in minor football leagues for three years before the Rams signed him in 1998 at 27 years old. On the day Warner made the team, Vermeil told him,

Left tackle Orlando Pace made seven Pro Bowls while playing for the Rams.

Receiver Torry Holt led the NFL in receiving yards twice with the Rams.

"Kurt, there's something special about you, and I can't wait to find out what it is."

With Green out, Warner was suddenly thrown into the fire. Many people thought the season was over before it even started. But Vermeil disagreed. In a press conference after Green's injury, the coach said, "We will rally around Kurt Warner, and we'll play good football."

"WE WILL RALLY AROUND KURT WARNER, AND WE'LL PLAY GOOD FOOTBALL."

—DICK VERMEIL

Even Vermeil couldn't have predicted how quickly Warner would take over the league. Warner was the most accurate passer in the NFL in 1999. That allowed offensive coordinator Mike Martz to unleash his many offensive weapons. Faulk led the league in total yards again while posting

Quarterback Kurt Warner made the Pro Bowl in three straight seasons starting in 1999.

more than 1,000 yards both rushing and receiving. Bruce caught 12 of Warner's NFL-best 41 touchdown passes. Fellow wide receivers Holt and Az-Zahir Hakim combined for 14 more scores.

The Rams piled up big numbers week after week on their way to a stunning 13–3 record. Along the way, they led the NFL by scoring 526 points. Before long, the Rams' indoor home stadium, the TWA Dome, was rocking. The high-powered offense was dubbed "the Greatest Show on Turf."

After the season, the awards rolled in. Warner was the NFL's MVP. Faulk was named the Offensive Player of the Year. The Rams' offensive firepower was on full display in the divisional round of the playoffs. Warner threw five touchdown passes to lead the Rams to a

ALL-AROUND RUNNING BACK

The Rams' offense played so well in 1999 that running back Marshall Faulk finished second in MVP voting behind only Kurt Warner. Faulk was equally effective as a runner and a pass catcher, so he played all over the field. That season, Faulk recorded 1,381 rushing yards and 1,048 receiving yards to lead the league in total yards for the second year in a row. He became just the second player in NFL history to have more than 1,000 rushing and receiving yards in one season.

Warner, *center*, set a Super Bowl record with 414 passing yards in Super Bowl XXXIV on January 30, 2000.

49–37 victory over the Minnesota Vikings. And when the Tampa Bay Buccaneers shut down the Rams' offensive show in the NFC title game, the defense stepped up to secure a hard-fought 11–6 victory and a trip to Super Bowl XXXIV.

THE TACKLE

In the Super Bowl, Warner threw all over the Tennessee Titans in the first half. But the Tennessee defense kept St. Louis out of the end zone and hit Warner frequently. The pressure didn't faze the quarterback, as he threw a 9-yard touchdown pass to Holt on the Rams' first drive of the second half.

The touchdown put the Rams ahead 16–0. After the score, Tennessee head coach Jeff Fisher noticed St. Louis players celebrating on the sideline as if the game was over. The Titans responded with three straight scoring drives to tie the game 16–16 with 2:12 left.

Instead of slowly moving the ball down the field to burn time off the clock, Martz called an aggressive play. All four Rams receivers ran deep routes, and Warner lofted a long pass toward Bruce. When the receiver caught the ball, a Tennessee defender slipped,

Receiver Isaac Bruce, *right*, runs down the field for a touchdown in the Super Bowl matchup between the Rams and the Tennessee Titans.

Rams linebacker Mike Jones tackles Titans receiver Kevin Dyson to help St. Louis win Super Bowl XXXIV.

and then Bruce cut past another defender to create a clear path to the end zone. The 73-yard touchdown put the Rams back in front just 18 seconds after the Titans tied the game.

However, this left plenty of time for the Titans to respond. And quarterback Steve McNair did just that, marching his team down the field to the Rams' 10-yard line. With only six seconds left, the fate of the Super Bowl came down to the final play.

McNair dropped back to pass and quickly threw to Titans wide receiver Kevin Dyson in the middle of the field. Rams linebacker Mike Jones was supposed to guard a different receiver, but when he realized Dyson had broken free over the middle of the field, Jones

quickly adjusted and ran toward Dyson. Dyson caught the ball at the 4-yard line, and Jones dived to wrap him up. While in Jones's grasp, Dyson desperately reached the ball toward the goal line. However, he fell inches short to seal the 23–16 victory for St. Louis. In a season defined by their explosive offense, the Rams won their first Super Bowl title thanks to an iconic defensive play.

STILL HUMMING

Following the emotional run to an unlikely Super Bowl title, Vermeil retired, and Martz took over as the Rams' head coach. While playing in the same offensive system, Warner proved his 1999 season wasn't a fluke. The Rams led the league in points again in 2000 and 2001.

Wide receiver Ricky Proehl (87) celebrates the Rams' only touchdown reception in Super Bowl XXXVI on February 3, 2002.

Thanks to their high-powered offense, St. Louis made it back to the Super Bowl after the 2001 regular season. Almost no one expected the underdog New England Patriots to keep the game close, let alone win. But New England head coach Bill Belichick designed a defensive plan to slow the Rams' passing attack. The Patriots held the Rams' offense in check and jumped out to a 17–3 lead.

New England could only slow down the Rams for so long. In the fourth quarter, Warner ran for a touchdown and threw for another to tie the game with 1:30 left. However, young Patriots quarterback Tom Brady led a late drive to set up a game-winning field goal to hand St. Louis a 20–17 loss. After experiencing the high of winning the Super Bowl on the final play two years earlier, the Rams now had to deal with the heartbreak of losing one in the game's final seconds.

Warner walks off the field after the New England Patriots shocked the Rams in Super Bowl XXXVI.

In 2002, Kurt Warner started six games and threw just three touchdowns.

CHAPTER 5

BACK TO THE WEST COAST

WITH MIKE MARTZ AND KURT WARNER LEADING THE TEAM, THE RAMS seemed poised for more success. However, Warner suffered multiple injuries in 2002 and 2003 that derailed each season. No longer confident in Warner's ability to stay healthy or perform as he did in the past, the team cut him before the 2004 season.

Another reason the Rams moved on from Warner was because of the performance of backup quarterback Marc Bulger. Bulger replaced Warner early in 2003, and he helped lead the Rams to the playoffs that season and in 2004. However, the team didn't make it past the divisional round either year. Then Martz missed 11 games in 2005 due to illness, and when the Rams finished 6–10 that season, he was fired. After Marshall Faulk retired in 2007, St. Louis was without several key members of the Greatest Show on Turf.

MOVING BACK

Running back Marshall Faulk was inducted into the Pro Football Hall of Fame in 2011.

The Rams spent the rest of the decade at the bottom of the standings. In 2009, they finished 1–15. As the losses piled up, fans grew frustrated with the direction of the team. Meanwhile, team owner Stan Kroenke, who took over in 2010, began planning to move the Rams out of St. Louis. When they originally moved to the city in 1995, the Rams signed an agreement that would keep them in St. Louis until 2015. And by then, the team was supposed to have one of the nicest stadiums in the league.

As that deadline approached, the city came up with a plan for a new stadium. But Kroenke ignored those plans. With an owner not dedicated to the city, and the Rams showing little signs of success, attendance plummeted for home games.

The Rams take the field for their first home game in California since 1994.

By the end of the 2015 season, the Rams had missed the playoffs for 11 straight years. With no agreed plan for a new stadium in St. Louis, Kroenke pushed to move the team back to Los Angeles. In January 2016, the move was approved, setting up the Rams to play in the Coliseum for the first time since 1979. Meanwhile, Kroenke began planning to build a new stadium in Inglewood, California, which was 12 miles (19 km) south of Los Angeles.

Defensive tackle Aaron Donald, *center*, won the NFL Defensive Player of the Year Award three times during his career.

BUILDING UP TALENT

The team arrived back in California in 2016 with a handful of new stars. The Rams had selected defensive tackle Aaron Donald in the first round of the 2014 draft. At 285 pounds, Donald was thought by many scouts to be too small to handle the larger offensive linemen in the NFL. But Donald made up for his lack of size with quick footwork and elite strength. Recording nine sacks during his first season, Donald won the NFL's Defensive Rookie of the Year Award.

One year later, the Rams drafted running back Todd Gurley from Georgia. The elusive Gurley showcased his skills by running for 1,106 yards and 10 touchdowns in 2015 to earn the Offensive Rookie of the Year Award. He became a staple for the Rams' offense for the next few years.

Despite their new talent, the Rams still lacked a standout quarterback. Before the 2016 draft, the Rams traded some picks in order to get the first overall selection. With it, the Rams grabbed quarterback Jared Goff to become the new face of the team. But Goff struggled as a rookie and threw only five touchdown passes in seven starts. The team lost all seven of those games and finished with a 4–12 record.

Heading into the 2017 season, the Rams looked to maximize Goff's potential by hiring Sean McVay as the team's head coach. At only 30 years old, McVay became the youngest NFL head coach since 1938. Despite his young age, McVay had plenty of experience. As the offensive coordinator for Washington the previous three seasons, McVay orchestrated one of the league's highest-scoring units.

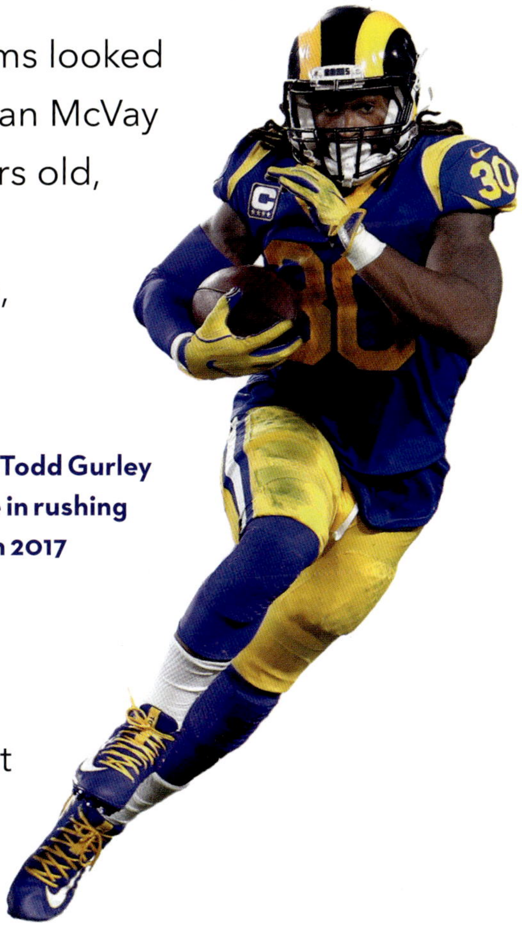

Running back Todd Gurley led the league in rushing touchdowns in 2017 and 2018.

Goff looked like a completely different quarterback under McVay. In a system that emphasized play-action passes,

Gurley and rookie receiver Cooper Kupp became Goff's go-to targets. A year after finishing with the league's lowest-scoring offense, the Rams led the NFL in points in 2017.

McVay helped Los Angeles end its 12-year playoff drought to win its division that year. Although the Rams lost in the opening round of the playoffs against the Atlanta Falcons, they built on that season's success and played even better in 2018. Behind their explosive offense, the Rams finished with a 13–3 record.

After beating the Dallas Cowboys at home, the Rams traveled to New Orleans to take on the Saints in the NFC title game. After the Saints jumped out to a 13–0 lead in the first quarter, Goff led the Rams to a comeback. He put together a late drive to get Los Angeles into field-goal range. Kicker Greg Zuerlein then booted a 48-yard field goal to tie the game 23–23 and send it into overtime.

The Saints started with the ball, giving New Orleans quarterback Drew Brees a chance to win the game. However, Rams safety John Johnson intercepted Brees near midfield. Goff then completed two passes to put Zuerlein in range for a game-winning field goal. The kicker drilled the ball 57 yards to win the game 26–23 and secure a spot for the Rams in Super Bowl LIII.

Head coach Sean McVay, *left*, talks to quarterback Jared Goff during a game in 2017.

Just as they had 18 years earlier, the Rams faced off with the New England Patriots in the Super Bowl on February 3, 2019. While Los Angeles was a completely different team, Bill Belichick and Tom Brady still led the Patriots and had established them as one of the league's most dominant franchises. New England kept the Rams out of the end zone and secured its sixth Super Bowl title by defeating Los Angeles 13–3. With the loss, the Rams became the first team in 47 years to not score a touchdown in the Super Bowl.

GOING ALL IN

Despite the poor performance in Super Bowl LIII, the Rams looked as though they could be contenders for years to come. However, Goff's play began to slip over the next

GAME FOR THE AGES

In Week 11 of the 2018 season, the Rams faced off against the Kansas City Chiefs in a highly anticipated matchup between the best offenses in the NFL that year. The back-and-forth game had Rams quarterback Jared Goff and Chiefs quarterback Patrick Mahomes combining for 891 passing yards and 10 touchdowns. But in a matchup that featured a ton of offense, Rams linebacker Samson Ebukam stole the show. Ebukam returned a fumble and an interception for touchdowns to help the Rams win 54–51.

Samson Ebukam returns a fumble in a 2018 game against the Kansas City Chiefs.

Goff, *left*, is hit by a New England defender during Super Bowl LIII in February 2019.

few seasons. While the Rams had a winning record in 2019 and 2020, McVay didn't believe Goff could lead the team to a Super Bowl title. Before the 2021 season, the Rams traded Goff to the Detroit Lions in exchange for veteran quarterback Matthew Stafford.

Stafford possessed a rocket of an arm and could make difficult throws. The Rams believed the quarterback was what they needed to send them over the top.

Along with Stafford, Los Angeles picked up several other key players. In 2019, the team acquired Pro Bowl cornerback Jalen Ramsey from the Jacksonville Jaguars. Then after starting 7–1 in 2021, the Rams traded with the Denver Broncos for superstar linebacker Von Miller.

All those moves paid off. Stafford had a career year in 2021 that he capped off with the clutch drive in Super Bowl LVI against the Cincinnati Bengals. On defense, Ramsey continued to shut down opposing receivers, while Miller's veteran presence showed up playing alongside Donald. Miller and Donald each recorded two sacks in the Super Bowl. With the Rams leading 23–20, Donald wrapped up Bengals quarterback Joe Burrow to force an incomplete pass. In a moment that symbolized the Rams as champions, Donald celebrated by pointing to the finger where he would put on his Super Bowl ring.

The Rams' aggressive trades led the team to a championship, but it came with a cost. Los Angeles didn't make a first-round pick from 2017 to 2023,

Donald celebrates his game-winning play to help the Rams secure their second Super Bowl title.

RAMS TROPHY CASE

SUPER BOWL CHAMPIONSHIPS: 2

Super Bowl XXXIV – January 30, 2000
Super Bowl LVI – February 13, 2022

NFL CHAMPIONSHIPS: 2

1945, 1951

CONFERENCE CHAMPIONSHIPS: 5

1979, 1999, 2001, 2018, 2021

DIVISION TITLES: 22

NFL West: 1945, 1949, 1950, 1951, 1955
NFL Coastal: 1967, 1969
NFC West: 1973, 1974, 1975, 1976, 1977, 1978, 1979, 1985, 1999, 2001, 2003, 2017, 2018, 2021, 2024

All stats are through the 2024 season.

limiting its chances to find future stars. Then after the 2023 season, Donald retired.

Linebacker Jared Verse won the NFL's Defensive Rookie of the Year Award in 2024.

Even with those hurdles, the team still found talent without high picks. In 2022, Los Angeles drafted running back Kyren Williams in the fifth round. The next year, the team selected wide receiver Puka Nacua. A physical player, Nacua broke two NFL rookie records by hauling in 105 receptions for 1,486 yards in 2023. Meanwhile, Williams led the league by averaging more than 95 rushing yards per game that year.

With Williams and Nacua assuming key roles on offense, the Rams made it back to the playoffs in 2023 and 2024. But they fell just short against the Lions the first year, losing 24–23. The next season, Los Angeles hosted the Minnesota Vikings in the wild-card round. Rookie defensive end Jared Verse recovered a fumble and scored a 57-yard touchdown to help the Rams win 27–9.

The Rams' season ended the following week in a 28–22 loss against the eventual Super Bowl–champion Philadelphia Eagles. Even so, few people had expected the young Los Angeles team to make it that far. With McVay leading a talented roster, the future looked bright for the Rams.

TIMELINE

1936
The Cleveland Rams play their first season in the AFL.

1937
The Rams join the NFL.

1945
In their last season in Cleveland, the Rams win the NFL Championship Game on December 16.

1946
The Rams move to Los Angeles, making them the first major pro team to play on the West Coast.

1951
The Rams defeat the Cleveland Browns in the NFL title game on December 23.

1973
In Chuck Knox's first season as coach, the Rams win their first of seven straight division titles.

1980
The Rams make their first Super Bowl appearance but lose to the Pittsburgh Steelers on January 20.

The Rams leave Los Angeles to play in St. Louis.
1995

2000
Quarterback Kurt Warner wins the MVP Award and leads the Rams to their first Super Bowl title on January 30.

In Super Bowl XXXVI on February 3, the New England Patriots upset the Rams on a last-second field goal.
2002

2016
After 21 seasons in St. Louis, the Rams move back to Los Angeles.

Under head coach Sean McVay, the Rams' offense is shut down by the Patriots in Super Bowl LIII on February 3.
2019

2022
Playing in their home stadium, the Rams win Super Bowl LVI on February 13.

GLOSSARY

backfield—the set of players, including quarterback and running backs, who line up behind the offensive line.

clutch—an important or pressure-packed situation.

coordinator—an assistant coach who is in charge of the offense, defense, or special teams.

draft—a system that allows teams to acquire new players coming into a league.

drought—a long period without success.

era—a period of time in history.

fluke—an unlikely event that occurs thanks to a stroke of luck.

franchise—an entire sports organization.

free agent—a player who is not signed to a team.

fumble—losing the ball and allowing the opponent a chance to recover it.

halfback pass—a play in which the running back has the option to throw the ball to a receiver.

interception—a pass that is caught by a defensive player.

offseason—the time of year when there are no games.

play-action pass—a play in which the quarterback fakes a handoff before dropping back to pass.

postseason—another word for playoffs; the time after the end of the regular season when teams play to determine a champion.

Pro Bowl—a postseason competition that the NFL's all-stars are invited to compete in.

retire—to end one's career.

rookie–a professional athlete in his or her first year of competition.

roster–a list of players who make up a team.

sack–a tackle of the quarterback behind the line of scrimmage before he can pass the ball.

scout–a person whose job is to look for talented young players.

segregate–to separate groups of people based on race, gender, ethnicity, or other factors.

turnover–loss of the ball to the other team through an interception or fumble.

veteran–someone who has played for many years.

ONLINE RESOURCES

Booklinks
NONFICTION NETWORK
FREE! ONLINE NONFICTION RESOURCES

To learn more about the Los Angeles Rams, please visit **abdobooklinks.com** or scan this QR code. These links are routinely monitored and updated to provide the most current information available.

INDEX